Self-Harm and Suicide

By Jillian Powell

Health Consultant: John G. Samanich, M.D.

Gareth Stevens
Publishing

A WEEKLY READER COMPANY

Please visit our web site at www.garethstevens.com.
For a free color catalog describing Gareth Stevens
Publishing's list of high-quality books, call
1-800-542-2595 (USA) or 1-800-387-3178 (Canada).
Gareth Stevens Publishing's fax: 1-877-542-2596

Library of Congress Cataloging in Publication Data
Powell, Jillian.
  Self-harm and suicide / Jillian Powell.
    p. cm. — (Emotional health issues)
  Includes bibliographical references and index.
  ISBN-10: 0-8368-9202-X (lib. bdg.)
  ISBN-13: 978-0-8368-9202-4 (lib. bdg.)
  1. Self-destructive behavior—Juvenile literature.
2. Parasuicide—Juvenile literature.   3. Suicide—Juvenile
literature.   I. Title.
  RC569.5.S45P69   2009
  616.85'82—dc22   2008004276

This North American edition first published in 2009 by
Gareth Stevens Publishing
A Weekly Reader® Company
1 Reader's Digest Road
Pleasantville, NY 10570-7000 USA

This U.S. edition copyright © 2009 by Gareth Stevens, Inc.
Original edition copyright © 2008 by Wayland. First published in Great Britain in 2008
by Wayland, 338 Euston Road, London NW1 3BH, United Kingdom.

Series Editor: Nicola Edwards   Consultant: Peter Evans
Designer: Alix Wood   Picture Researcher: Kathy Lockley

Gareth Stevens Managing Editor: Lisa M. Herrington
Gareth Stevens Senior Editor: Barbara Bakowski
Gareth Stevens Creative Director: Lisa Donovan

Photo credits: Ace Stock/Alamy Images: 17; Mark Baigent/Alamy Images: 23;
Paul Baldesare/Photofusion Picture Library: 10; Mark J. Barrett/Alamy Images: 25;
Jaubert Bernard/Alamy Images: Cover, 21; George Blonsky/Alamy Images: title page, 36;
Trygve Bolstad/Panos Pictures: 42; Bubbles Photolibrary/Alamy Images:15, 19;
Comstock Select/Corbis:13t; Simon Cowling/Alamy Images: 4; Jo Giron/Corbis: 35;
Richard Green/Alamy Images: 7; Steve Hamblin/Alamy Images: 40; Ute Klaphake/Photofusion
Picture Library: 24; Kolvenbach/Alamy Images: 26; Mediscan/Corbis: 34; Charlie Newham/
Alamy Images: 8; Christian Schmidt/zefa/ Corbis: 32; Tom Stewart/Corbis: 38; Thinkstock/Corbis:13b;
Jim West/Alamy Images: 44; David White/Alamy Images: 14; Terry Whittaker/Alamy Images: 45;
Janine Wiedel Photolibrary/Alamy Images: 37; Wayland Archive: 16, 20, 28, 30

Printed in China
1 2 3 4 5 6 7 8 9 10 09 08

The information in this book is not intended to substitute for professional medical or psychological care. The case studies are based on real experiences, but the names are fictitious. All people in the photos are models except where a caption specifically names an individual.

Contents

Words that appear in **boldface** type are in the
glossary on page 46.

Introduction

Jemma has been cutting her arm. She uses the blade from a razor. Jemma doesn't know why she cuts herself.

She just knows that the feeling builds and builds inside her until cutting is her only release. When she is cutting, she feels as if she can breathe again. Afterward, she feels ashamed and guilty. She has to wear long sleeves to hide the cuts on her arms.

People sometimes use razor blades for cutting, a practice that carries a risk of infection.

Jemma is self-harming. Self-harm means deliberately hurting or injuring oneself. It can take many forms, such as cutting, scratching, or burning the skin, pulling out hair or eyelashes, or punching and bruising oneself. Other forms of self-harm include deliberately engaging in risky behavior, such as practicing unsafe sex, smoking or drinking heavily, **inhaling** substances, or abusing **prescribed** or illegal drugs.

Self-harm

In the past three decades, self-harm has become more common among children and young people. Statistics from around the world suggest that as many as one in ten young people practices self-harm. Actual figures may be even higher, because many cases go unreported. Self-harm is most common among teens. The average age at which someone starts self-harming is between 12 and 14. However, self-injury has been reported in children as young as four.

Suicide

Suicide is also increasing among children and teens. In the United States, it is the third leading cause of death in people ages 10 to 24. According to the U.S. Centers for Disease Control and Prevention, suicide accounts for almost 13 percent of deaths annually among 15- to 24-year-olds. In 2005, about 17 percent of students in grades 9 to 12 said they had "seriously considered" suicide. Although girls are more likely than boys to attempt suicide, boys are more likely to die by completed suicide.

Coping with emotions

Suicide and self-harm are different, although they are related. Both are ways of dealing with strong emotions. Both reflect a feeling of low **self-esteem**. Self-harm is not usually an attempt at suicide, however. It is an attempt to cope with feelings of pain and distress. Suicide can be a reaction to hopelessness and despair. It is a way of bringing to an end feelings that are too painful to bear. Many people self-harm for years without attempting suicide, but suicide can sometimes follow self-harm. People with a long-term habit of self-harm are at greater risk of attempting suicide.

Find out more

This book gives you the facts about self-harm and suicide. It explains the causes and risk factors for self-injury and suicide and identifies the impacts on young people and their families.

The book considers why self-harm and suicide are increasing among children and teens; offers advice on ways to seek help; and shows that young people can overcome problems and learn to find other means of coping with crises in their lives.

It's a fact: self-harm and suicide

- About 3 million Americans, most of them teenagers, practice self-harm.

- In one recent study, almost 14 percent of high school students surveyed said they had self-harmed. One in four of them had begun the practice by the sixth grade.

- Each year, about 32,000 Americans die by suicide. Almost 5,000 of them are under the age of 24.

- Each day, 14 people between the ages of 15 and 24 die by suicide. That is one young person every 100 minutes.

5

Chapter 1: *Depression and other mental disorders*

Both self-harm and suicide reflect underlying problems of **depression.** Most people feel sad or depressed sometimes. Feeling sad is a normal reaction when a person experiences events that are upsetting or stressful. During **puberty**, emotions are affected by chemicals in the body called **hormones.** These chemicals can alter mood, sometimes causing mood swings and making a young person feel sad and tearful or angry and upset.

It's a fact: problems with mental health

- One in four people worldwide will have mental health problems at some time during his or her life.

- Serious emotional disturbances affect one in every ten young people at any given time.

- One in eight teens has depression.

Temporary mood swings are normal and usually pass. When overwhelming sadness goes on for months and begins to affect home and school life, however, a young person may need professional help and treatment. Some teens are more likely to develop mental health problems because of **genetic** factors. External stresses—things that are happening in their lives that make them feel unhappy or anxious—can combine with genetic factors to lead to depression.

Rising mental health disorders

Recent studies show that depression and other mental health problems are increasing among children and young people. The World Health Organization (WHO) and the United Nations

Doctors are seeing a growing number of children and young people with stress-related illnesses and depression.

Children's Fund (UNICEF) recently warned that up to one in five of the world's children has mental health or behavioral problems. This figure includes children living in developed countries as well as in developing nations and war zones.

More girls than boys have emotional disorders, such as **eating disorders**. More boys have behavioral disorders, such as **attention-deficit/hyperactivity disorder** (ADHD). Some mental disorders are temporary. Others can become long-term problems that lead to academic failure, self-harm, alcohol and drug abuse, or suicide.

Antidepressants

An increasing number of children and teenagers are being treated with medications called **antidepressants**.

These drugs affect mood by altering the balance of chemicals in the brain. Some medical professionals and others have raised concerns about an increased risk of suicidal thoughts and behavior in children and teens who are taking antidepressants. The U.S. Food and Drug Administration requires a printed warning on the label of all antidepressant medications regarding their use by people under the age of 24.

Some people say the rise in the number of children and teens being diagnosed with depression and other mental health disorders is the result of better methods of diagnosis and improved understanding of mental health. Other people say the increase reflects the growing pressures and stresses on young people today.

Social changes and causes

Being a child today is very different from being a child in previous generations. Many experts believe that the rise in depression and mental health problems among children is due to new stresses and pressures young people face. These stresses come from changes in society and the family as well as from pressures at school. Another source of stress is the influence of the media, such as magazines, television, and the Internet.

Changes in the family

In the United States, where about half of all marriages end in divorce, one study found that 20 to 25 percent of children suffered long-term depression after their parents' split. According to U.S. Census Bureau estimates, 59 percent of children will live in a single-parent home at least once during their youth. Although many children in single-parent households grow up without experiencing problems, they are twice as likely as children in two-parent families to have mental health disorders. This difference may reflect the difficulties that some parents have coping alone with financial and other challenges. Children living in stepfamilies are also more likely to experience depression and other mental health problems.

Exam pressures

At school, children face increased academic pressures. In many countries, students are being tested at younger ages than ever before. Student surveys show that academic pressure is one of the greatest sources of stress among teens. Admission to colleges and universities has become increasingly competitive, and many young people are struggling to achieve high

An increasingly competitive job market puts young people under more pressure to attain high educational qualifications.

CASE STUDY

Thirteen-year-old Lauren had been feeling unhappy since her parents divorced two years earlier. She still cried when she thought about the day they told her of their decision. Although she saw her dad on most weekends, she missed him terribly. Family life at home got worse when her mom's new boyfriend, Daniel, moved in. He was much stricter than her dad had been. Daniel grounded Lauren for the smallest offense. Lauren resented him because he was not her dad; she felt that Daniel was trying to take her father's place. Her mother always seemed to take Daniel's side, making Lauren feel like an outsider in her own home. Lauren did not tell her dad because she didn't want to cause more trouble between her parents.

She often had headaches and stomachaches and began missing many days of school. With exams coming up, Lauren was feeling a lot of pressure. Her marks had been sliding, and her teachers were disappointed in her performance. Lauren felt that everything in her life was spinning out of control. She called a teen helpline because she felt desperate to talk to someone about her problems.

standards of performance. They worry that they will not meet their parents' and their own expectations.

Bullying

Bullying is a major problem among young people. With the growth of Internet use, there has been a rise in bullying that takes place through text messages, in e-mails, and on web sites. Approximately 5 million children in the United States, or one in seven, are affected as either a bully or a victim. Constant bullying can cause low self-esteem, a major factor in self-harm and suicide. Research by the American Academy of Child and Adolescent Psychiatry shows that young people who are victims of bullying are at increased risk of suicidal thoughts and behavior. Being bullied can overwhelm a young person who is facing other problems, too, such as a family breakup or the death of a relative or friend.

Teen consumers

Advertisers target children and teens as consumers. Media images often show slim and glamorous models. Young people, whose bodies are changing during puberty, may feel that they do not measure up to media portrayals. These teens can develop a poor **body image** and experience low self-esteem. Images of ultra-thin models and celebrities can encourage healthy young people to feel that they are overweight. Such feelings may lead to eating disorders such as **anorexia nervosa** and **bulimia nervosa**.

Chapter 2: *Self-harm—the facts*

Self-harm is also called self-injury. People deliberately harm themselves in many different ways. The most common way is by cutting. Usually they cut their arms or legs, but they may cut any part of the body, such as the face or the chest.

Self-harm methods

Most self-harmers use knives, razor blades, glass, or other sharp objects. Sometimes they scratch the skin with fingernails, combs, or knives or deliberately pick at scars to reopen wounds. Burning or scalding the skin with cigarettes and matches is another method of self-harm. Some people scrub their skin with harsh substances like bleach, or they pull out their hair or eyelashes. Others bang their heads or throw themselves against walls hard enough to cause bruises. People who self-harm may punch or hit themselves. Some people may even use bricks or hammers to break bones in their arms or legs. Other forms of self-harm include swallowing inedible objects and inhaling dangerous substances.

Young people often feel immune to risks and deliberately rebel against health warnings.

Risky behavior

People can also self-harm through deliberately risky behavior. Risky behavior can be a way of trying to block out anxiety or unhappiness by providing temporary relief from unwanted feelings. Young people may skip school or shoplift with their friends. They may experiment with dangerous, and sometimes deadly, activities such as reckless driving or "car surfing"—hanging on to or standing on top of a moving vehicle.

Young people also take risks by practicing unprotected sex. This behavior increases the risk of contracting sexually transmitted infections and diseases, including **human immunodeficiency virus** (HIV), the virus that causes **acquired immune deficiency syndrome** (AIDS).

People who self-harm may also smoke heavily or engage in **binge drinking**, putting their health at risk. Using drugs recklessly is another form of self-harm. Drug **overdose** is the most common cause of hospital admissions for self-harm.

Some people who self-injure have mental health problems such as **obsessive-compulsive disorder** (OCD) or eating disorders. Some studies indicate that about one-quarter of young people with eating disorders cut themselves or practice other forms of self-harm.

CASE STUDY

Sofia was 14 when she started self-harming. She was at a big family gathering after her grandmother's funeral. Sofia had adored her grandmother and had felt that Nana was the only person in whom she could confide.

While other family members and friends were talking and eating, Sofia locked herself in a bathroom upstairs. She noticed a razor lying on the side of the bathtub. Something made her pick it up and cut the back of her hand. Somehow she felt that she was shutting out everyone else at the funeral and every event that was happening. Seeing her own blood made her feel more real and alive. The physical pain came as a relief from the heartache she had felt since Nana's death.

Sofia didn't tell anyone about the cutting. Soon she did it again. She began locking herself in the bathroom and pretending to take long baths. She was addicted to the "rush" and the relief that she remembered from the day of the funeral.

Who self-harms?

People of every age, race, and background self-harm. Girls are more likely than boys to self-harm. However, instances of self-harm among men and boys have doubled since the 1980s.

Young women between the ages of 15 and 19 are most at risk of practicing self-harm, as are young men between the ages of 20 and 24. College counselors report growing numbers of students asking for help because they are self-harming. In a recent study of college students, 18 percent said they had harmed themselves more than 10 times.

Self-harming sessions usually take place in private, in bathrooms or bedrooms.

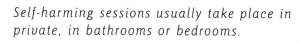

It's a fact:
self-harm

- A recent study of 15- and 16-year-olds showed that girls are four times as likely as boys to self-harm.

- American Indians and Native Alaskans have higher rates of self-harm than other ethnic groups.

- Young people who abuse alcohol or drugs such as marijuana and cocaine are more likely to self-harm than those who do not have substance-abuse problems.

Current research indicates that about 15 percent of high school students have self-harmed. The problem is becoming more common among younger teens and children, too. Some mental health professionals call self-harm a "hidden epidemic" among young people.

Some groups of children and teens are at greater risk for self-harm than others. Children with mental health problems or learning difficulties are more likely to self-harm, as are those who have experienced **physical abuse** or **sexual abuse**. Young people who are homeless, in foster care, or in juvenile detention centers have higher rates of self-harm. Risk is also greater for young people in families where there are problems such as alcoholism, untreated mental illness, financial stress, and domestic violence.

Overwhelming problems

Some young people self-harm only once or twice, as an impulsive reaction to extreme stress or anguish. They might bang their heads or punch their fists against a wall because they feel angry, frustrated, or upset.

For other teenagers, self-harm can develop into a way of coping with their problems. It becomes something they do every week or even every day.

For these teens, self-injury is a means of blotting out difficult circumstances or emotions that they deal with on an everyday basis. They may also turn to cutting or other self-harm behaviors when something triggers memories of a painful experience or event.

People who self-harm are likely to be depressed and worried. They may be overwhelmed by the problems in their lives and think they are unable to cope. They may blame themselves for their problems and be unable to seek help from family or friends.

Self-harm can sometimes be an impulsive act, in sudden response to anger or frustration.

Why do some people self-harm?

Self-harm is a way of coping with very difficult or painful feelings. During the act of cutting or burning, for example, people can experience a temporary relief or release from their bad feelings. They may feel as if the physical pain briefly blots out their mental pain. After self-harming, however, they often feel guilty and upset that they have resorted to injuring themselves.

Feeling addicted

Self-harm can have different effects on different people. Some people say the sensation of pain makes them feel aware and alive. It stimulates them out of depression, emotional numbness, or hopelessness. Other people say they feel a sense of **detachment** when they self-harm. Self-harm is habit-forming. Some experts believe it may be physically addictive. When the body is injured, it releases painkilling chemicals. Many people who develop long-term self-injury behavior find that they have to self-harm more often and more severely to achieve the same sense of relief they once did.

Experiencing abuse

Some people self-harm because they feel their behavior gives them control and ownership of their bodies. This is often true of people who have been physically or sexually abused. Children who have been abused may feel that they have no control over what happened to their bodies. They may also feel a deep sense of shame and guilt that they were unable to stop the abuse, even though it was not their

Actress Angelina Jolie has spoken about cutting herself when she was a teen. She said that being teased and feeling rejected led to depression and then to self-harm.

fault. Abused children may feel disgust for their bodies. Self-harm becomes a form of punishment or a way of expressing the disgust and guilt they have been made to feel.

Keeping self-harm secret

Once people begin to self-harm regularly, they can find it difficult to stop. They may feel guilty or ashamed and be unable to talk about their behavior. For this reason, self-harm is not usually a way of seeking attention from others. In fact, cutting and other forms of self-injury often remain hidden. Most people self-harm when they are alone and then hide any evidence that they have hurt themselves.

Some self-harmers have described the behavior as a way of having their "own space." Others have described it as "screaming silently, so no one else will hear." They see self-harm as a way of dealing with their problems on their own instead of turning to others for help. People who self-harm may go to great lengths to conceal their behavior.

People who self-harm may wear clothes that cover up the signs of injury, keeping their behavior a secret from others.

In focus: expressing pain

The idea of expressing inner pain on the outside of the body can be traced to a long tradition in religion and ancient cultures. Wearing a hair shirt, uncomfortably rough to the skin, and covering the head or body with ash were once done to express deep feelings of shame or penitence. Some ethnic groups still use ash or body paint during periods of mourning to express the pain of bereavement and their feelings of grief.

What causes self-harm?

Experts say that self-harm is linked to low self-esteem, or self-worth. Self-esteem is affected by the things that happen to a person and the way others behave toward him or her.

If a teenager has positive experiences in school and enjoys good relationships with family and friends, his or her self-esteem may improve. If a close relationship ends or the student fails an exam, his or her self-esteem may suffer.

Young people can bury the pain of abuse deep inside themselves, leading to feelings of loneliness and isolation.

Some people feel bad about themselves all the time. They may feel that they are "losers" and that others don't value or care for them. They may blame themselves for their failures or feel that they have let others down. Low self-esteem can lead to depression. It can also lead to self-harm.

Low self-esteem can develop in someone who is criticized, ignored, teased, or bullied regularly. For example, children who are routinely compared to high-achieving siblings may develop low self-esteem. They may worry constantly about letting themselves and their families down.

Bullying and abuse

Young people who have been bullied or abused are more likely to experience low self-esteem. Victims of bullying and abuse feel that their opinions and emotions are not valued or important. Sometimes they feel powerless to improve their situations.

A child may be bullied at school or at home, by a classmate, a teacher, a parent, a stepparent, or a sibling. The bully may focus on any number of characteristics—appearance, voice, race, or religion, for example.

Abuse can be emotional (such as name-calling and threats), physical, or sexual. Neglect, or failing to care for a child's basic needs such as clean clothes and adequate food, is the most common form of abuse.

Children and young people who experience abuse are four times as likely as others to self-harm. They may feel that they can control the pain of self-harm, unlike the pain they suffered as a result of abuse. Some studies have shown that frequent or long-term abuse was linked to a greater risk of self-harm behaviors.

Some students who are bullied at home become bullies at school, taking out their hurt and anger on others.

It's a fact: bullying

- Each year, nearly one in six students in grades six to 10 is a victim of bullying.

- In a study by the National Crime Prevention Council, 43 percent of teens said they had been bullied online.

- Girls are as likely as boys to be bullied physically.

Body image and self-harm

For most young people, body image is an important part of self-esteem. Body image is the way a person feels about his or her physical appearance. In a survey of 10,000 teens, slightly more than half of the boys and about two-thirds of the girls were unhappy with their bodies. One-third of teens would consider cosmetic surgery to improve their body shape. Two out of three girls under the age of 13 have dieted.

Although teenage girls are most affected, boys and young men increasingly report poor body image. They compare themselves to idealized advertising and other media images, and they feel under pressure to have similarly muscular and toned bodies.

Children and teens who have physical disabilities or scars from accidents can also develop low self-esteem because of poor body image.

Celebrity icons

Many people believe that young people are becoming more concerned with body image because they are surrounded by images of ultra-slim celebrities and models. Children grow up believing that others will judge them on how they look. If they feel they fail to measure up, their poor body image can lead to self-harm.

It's a fact: super-skinny models

- Most photographs of fashion models are altered to create an ideal but unrealistic appearance.

- Twenty years ago, models weighed 8 percent less than other women, on average. Today, models weigh about 23 percent less than other women.

- A survey of 2,000 teenage girls found that although 19 percent of them were overweight, 67 percent *thought* they were too heavy.

- About 80 percent of girls and women say they have low self-esteem after looking at fashion magazines.

Teenagers can become obsessed with body weight, sometimes alternating between dieting and turning to food for comfort.

CASE STUDY

Michelle frequently read celebrity and fashion magazines and wished she could look like the models and celebrities in the photos. She envied their slender figures and glamorous appearances. Michelle hated the way she looked. Puberty had brought acne and an increase in body fat. She thought that all her friends were slimmer and prettier than she was. When they went out to clubs, she was always the one left standing on her own. One night, Michelle overheard a boy call her "the fat one." She felt devastated. She didn't tell her friends, but she was stung by the remark.

Although Michelle tried to diet, she enjoyed food and just could not help eating for comfort when she was feeling down. Sometimes she ate a whole box of cookies and then felt upset and angry with herself. She hated herself and felt that others hated her, too. Michelle began scratching her arms with pins because it felt like a way of punishing herself and relieving some emotional pain.

Substance abuse and self-harm

Some people use alcohol or other drugs to self-harm. Most people admitted to hospitals for self-harm have taken a drug overdose. Half of all men and one-fourth of all women admitted to hospitals for self-harm have been drinking alcohol.

Teens who abuse alcohol and drugs are more likely than others to engage in high-risk behaviors. These acts include having unprotected sex, fighting, failure to use seat belts, and riding with a driver who has been drinking alcohol.

Alcohol abuse

Young people who abuse alcohol are more likely to self-harm. Underage drinking is a problem in many countries. In the United States, people younger than 21 are not legally allowed to drink alcohol. Yet every year, thousands of children and teenagers are admitted to hospitals for **alcohol poisoning**.

Studies in the United States show that young people who abuse alcohol risk long-term physical and mental damage. Yet more and more young people are regularly binge drinking (consuming five or more alcoholic drinks within a short period). The National Survey on Drug Use and Health released in 2007 showed that more than 42 percent of people ages 18 to 25 in the United States reported binge drinking at least once a month. About one in ten 12- to 17-year-olds said they engaged in binge drinking.

Young people may not realize the alcohol content of the drinks they consume. Alcohol poisoning can lead to loss of consciousness and sometimes even death.

In focus: overdosing

A drug overdose is the accidental or intentional use of a drug in a higher amount than is prescribed or normally used. Even drugs generally considered safe can cause serious health consequences when taken in excessive amounts.

Acetaminophen is a common over-the-counter medicine used to reduce fever and relieve pain. An overdose of acetaminophen can result in liver and kidney damage. The drug is a most common method of self-poisoning in some countries, especially among teenage girls and young women.

The ready availability of painkillers makes them the most common means of self-poisoning.

Drug dangers

Young people, as well as older people who are self-harming for the first time, are most likely to take an overdose of an over-the-counter medicine, such as **acetaminophen**. People with a long-term habit of self-harm are more likely to overdose on prescribed medications, such as antidepressants or **tranquilizers**.

Young people who abuse illegal drugs are more likely to practice self-injury, and boys are twice as likely as girls to use illegal drugs to harm themselves. Doctors warn that drugs such as marijuana and Ecstasy can affect brain function, dulling people's abilities to think, concentrate, and remember.

Drug abuse can also lead to a variety of mental health problems, including depression, anxiety, and **paranoia**. Individuals with paranoia are overly suspicious, cautious, and secretive. They may believe that others are watching them or talking about them. Research also links drug use to the development of a severe mental illness called **schizophrenia**, in which a person withdraws from reality and has illogical, confused thoughts.

Youth subcultures

Many young people feel the need to belong to a smaller group or subculture within society. They express their personality or identity by associating with others who like the same things, such as styles of clothing or types of music. Group identity can also include marking the body with **tattoos** and **piercings**. Some youth subcultures, such as goths and emos (fans of a kind of music that displays strong emotion) have been linked with high rates of self-harm and suicide. These subcultures can glamorize the ideas of loneliness, unhappiness, and death. Many experts think subcultures may attract self-harmers who seek support among like-minded peers.

Self-harm and music

Recent studies suggest a link between self-harm and heavy metal, blues, and emo music. Some emo bands show people cutting on their album covers. There is also a growing genre of self-harm lyrics and music. Goth rockers such as Marilyn Manson have been criticized for appearing to glorify self-harm. Manson, who cuts himself with broken glass on stage, is said to have hundreds of scars on his body from self-harm.

In focus: self-harm circles

Most people self-harm when they are alone. It is a private, even secret, activity. Some teenagers, however, belong to groups of people within or outside school who practice self-harm. The members send each other text messages when they have self-harmed and often exchange pictures of scars. Some members even get together when they are cutting. Others join self-harm communities on the Internet and communicate through chat rooms or message boards.

Copycat behavior

Some studies suggest that young people may be encouraged to engage in "copycat" behavior by hearing about celebrities or seeing familiar characters in television shows who self-harm. Teenagers are also more likely to self-harm if they have a relative or a friend who does it.

Health-care professionals have called for caution in the reporting of self-harm activities by celebrities. Experts say that teenagers who are going through a difficult time can be influenced by these celebrity stories. Some teens may see self-harm as an appropriate way of dealing with their problems.

Self-harm web sites

Many web sites about self-harm offer a valuable source of information and support for teenagers and their families. Some people fear, however, that such sites make self-harm behavior seem commonplace and may even encourage vulnerable young people to self-harm.

Research has found that some message boards include content that might reinforce or promote self-harm. Members sometimes post pictures of their injuries and scars. They exchange music tracks and poems about self-harm. Some web sites even offer merchandise, such as T-shirts and bracelets, that expresses membership in a self-injury club.

Message boards and chat rooms provide a forum for young people to talk with others going through similar experiences.

Chapter 3: *Self-harm treatment*

Most people who self-harm want to stop but don't know how. They may feel that hurting themselves is the only way they can cope with their feelings. Certain techniques, however, can help young people prevent or stop destructive behavior. Identifying possible causes of emotional pain and triggers of self-harm activities can be valuable.

Some people find it helpful to keep a mood diary or journal. Writing about their feelings can help them see how various events affect their mood. Recognizing the events and emotions that can trigger self-harm is a big step toward stopping the pattern of behavior.

Another beneficial exercise is to write a list of reasons against self-harming. Some people write a dialogue between one speaker who wants to self-harm and another who wants to stop.

Keeping a diary can provide an outlet for feelings and also help in recognizing patterns of thought and behavior.

In focus: *seeing blood*

Many young people who self-harm by cutting say that the sight of blood represents the flow of bad feelings and stress out of their bodies. Others say the blood is a substitute for the tears they can't cry. When they bleed, they experience relief and calm. One self-help technique recommended by therapists is to mark the skin temporarily, for example with a lipstick or a red felt-tip marker.

Distractions

Distraction techniques can help some teenagers avoid acting on the urge to self-harm. They might phone a friend, listen to music, play a sport, or go for a walk. Exercise can help because it causes the release of natural **endorphins** in the body. Endorphins are substances in the brain that can improve mood.

Creative activities, such as writing poetry, painting, and drawing, can also act as an outlet for feelings. One way of expressing a strong emotion such as anger is to create an abstract painting of shapes or a self-portrait in blacks and reds.

Coping strategies

If feelings of anger and frustration build up, it can help to express them physically by punching into a pile of pillows or a punching bag. Another method is to use relaxation techniques, such as slow breathing or counting from 10 down to zero.

There are other ways of making the body feel "harmless" pain that does not cause lasting injury. Teens may find it helpful to hold an ice cube against the skin, let an elastic band slap hard against a wrist, or bite into a strongly flavored food. Some people mark their skin with a pen or place adhesive bandages on the parts of their bodies that they feel the urge to injure.

Taking part in sports can enhance people's mood as well as improve their physical health.

Getting help

Many people who self-harm need help and support to stop. Because self-harm can be a very lonely problem, it is important that young people talk to someone they can trust. That person may be a family member, a friend, a teacher, a school nurse, or a guidance counselor. In many cases, those individuals will be able to listen and give advice in confidence. In circumstances where a young person may be in immediate danger, however, they need to act on the information to see that the teen gets the help he or she needs. Several support organizations have telephone hotlines and provide information and guidance (see page 47).

Taking the first step

The first stage in getting help is often an appointment with the family doctor. Doctors will assess the seriousness of the problem and

Telephone helplines can provide people with immediate support and advice in times of crisis. Turn to page 47 for a list of helplines that people at risk of self-harm and suicide can contact.

In focus: peer support

Many young people feel more comfortable confiding in someone of their own age. In peer support groups, young people are trained by professional counselors to listen in confidence to teens who face problems such as bullying, abuse, and self-harm.

suggest a range of therapies, which may include individual or family counseling, **psychotherapy,** and medication to relieve anxiety and depression. Doctors generally provide emergency contact information so that young people who repeatedly self-harm can seek immediate help during a crisis.

If self-harm behavior becomes life-threatening, a teen may need to be hospitalized. Most hospital admissions for self-harm are for drug overdoses.

Therapy

People who self-harm need to deal with the problems that are causing their unhappiness. Some people may feel that they are to blame for everything that has gone wrong in their lives. They need help to change their way of thinking about themselves and about the events they have experienced.

Teenagers with depression may be referred to psychologists or psychiatrists who are experienced in treating people who self-harm. Some of these experts work at specialized clinics. They listen to patients and help them understand their feelings and manage their emotions in a different way. These professionals may encourage young people to keep diaries and journals. Therapists may also suggest other outlets for expressing strong emotions.

It may also be helpful for a young person to join a local or online self-help group. People who share the same problems meet regularly to talk and support one another. Many young people feel more comfortable talking to their peers. Peer support programs in schools can offer another valuable source of help.

It's a fact:
recovery from self-harm

- Some people reach a point where they no longer feel the need to self-harm. Others find different coping strategies to help them get through times of crisis.

- Talking with a trusted individual is the first step toward recovery.

- Most people who cut themselves are not attempting suicide. It is possible for self-harm to result in accidental death, however. It is also possible for both suicidal thoughts and self-harm behaviors to exist in one person.

- People who self-harm regularly are more likely to attempt suicide than people who do not self-harm.

Family support

Many young people who self-harm try to keep their behavior secret from their families. Often, they harm when they are alone, and they take care to hide the evidence. Some young people eventually confide in a family member. In other cases, parents or siblings accidentally discover the behavior. They may see scars. Sometimes family members notice signs, such as clothing meant to cover up cuts or burns. Parents or siblings may find razors, knives, or scissors hidden in bedrooms. They may accidentally catch the young person in the act of self-injury. Family members can feel shocked, upset, and bewildered when they uncover a teen's self-harm.

Someone to listen

A parent or sibling should not shout, become angry, judge, or criticize a young person who is self-harming. That type of reaction will make the child or teenager feel more upset and alone. Issuing threats and extracting promises to stop self-harm behavior are not helpful tactics. A teen who promises not to self-harm and then fails to keep that pledge may feel guilty and may be less likely to confide

Giving an ultimatum to a teenager in an attempt to stop self-harm can make the teen feel more alone. He or she may be less likely to confide in others.

CASE STUDY

When Amy's ten-year-old brother, Cory, found her self-harming, he felt worried and upset. Amy was alarmed that Cory had caught her cutting her arms, and she shouted at him for bursting into her room. Amy made him promise not to tell their mother about the cutting. Cory couldn't understand why Amy would want to hurt herself; she was smart, pretty, and popular. He asked her why she was cutting herself, but she told him he was too young to be able to understand.

Cory felt awkward and embarrassed when their mother commented on Amy's long sleeves on a hot day. He felt torn. He knew that Amy was cutting herself when she shut herself away in her room. Cory knew that their mother would be angry if she learned that he hadn't revealed his sister's behavior. Amy made him promise not to tell, though, and he was worried that telling his mother would cause more trouble in the family. One day, he saw an article about self-harm in a magazine. He decided to find out more information on the Internet. He found a lot of useful web sites and printed some pages for Amy. He told her that she wasn't alone and suggested that they tell their mother together.

again. People who self-harm often feel worse when others attempt to control their behavior. Some self-harmers feel powerless or worthless and are trying to gain control over an area of their lives. They need help from people who will allow them to talk about their feelings and who will listen to them in a caring way.

Sometimes a brother or a sister can help by offering to find out information, talk to an adult about the self-harm, or be with the sibling when he or she tells a parent or seeks help. In some cases, a sibling may need to get first-aid help (such as wound care). A person with serious injuries needs immediate medical attention.

Family therapy

In some cases, doctors suggest family therapy. Therapy sessions include the young person as well as other members of the family. During family therapy, the child or teen can talk about his or her problems and unhappiness. The sessions help family members understand the child's feelings and work out strategies for making make positive changes.

Chapter 4: *Suicide—the facts*

In general, suicide rates have been rising around the world, especially among young people. The World Health Organization reports a 60 percent increase in suicides in the last 50 years. Some countries have much higher rates than others.

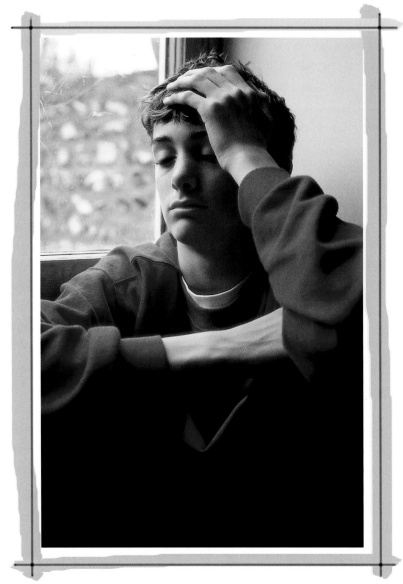

In many countries, teenage boys are among the highest-risk groups for suicide.

Rates of suicide

A recent report by the Organization for Economic Cooperation and Development lists Korea, Hungary, and Japan as the member countries with the highest rates of suicide. The United States recorded 10.2 suicides per 100,000 people, less than half Korea's figure. Largely Muslim countries, such as Jordan and Syria, where suicide is forbidden on religious grounds, have the lowest reported rates.

In the United States, suicide is the third most common cause of death among people ages 10 to 24. Girls are more likely to attempt suicide, but boys are more likely to die as a result of completed suicide. The use of firearms, a particularly deadly method, is most common among

It's a fact: suicide

- Most suicides in the United States involve the use of firearms.

- About four times as many men and boys as women and girls die by suicide.

- Women and girls are three times as likely as men and boys to attempt suicide.

- In the United States, the suicide rate among young people has tripled since the 1950s.

men and boys. In the United States, suffocation by hanging is the most common suicide method among girls ages 10 to 19. Girls have a greater chance of recovery if emergency treatment is given in time.

The rise of suicide sites

The Internet has begun a new trend for group suicides among the young. In Japan, which has a high rate of suicide (more than 30,000 people a year), the number of "Internet suicides" has more than doubled in recent years. Young people with suicidal feelings contact others on the Internet to plan and carry out group suicides, often by using poisonous substances or inhaling car exhaust fumes. Most suicide sites appear to be frequented largely by young people, some in their early teens. Many of them are troubled by bullying, romantic breakups, abuse, or family problems.

Feelings of despair

Young people who have attempted suicide report feelings of anxiety, loneliness, and hopelessness. Low self-esteem and feelings of powerlessness or failure are common factors. Some suicidal teens have long-term depression. Others have experienced a **trauma**, such as a family break-up or the death of a loved one.

Some young people were self-harming before they attempted suicide. Many experience difficulties at school or engage in criminal behavior. Other factors include physical or sexual abuse, unwanted pregnancy, drug or alcohol problems, and poverty.

People who are suicidal may feel unable to reach out for help. Young people who are considering taking their own lives often have the false belief that others will be better off without them.

Who is at risk?

Some research suggests that half of all young people who attempt suicide have a history of self-harm. Other studies show that impulsive behavior can be an important factor in suicides in this age group. In one study, one-fourth of suicides among young men were related to problems with close relationships soon before their deaths.

Ethnic origins

Some groups of young people have higher suicide rates than others. Cultural and ethnic origins can be factors. A study in the United Kingdom found that suicide is three times as likely in young Asian women as in white British women. In the United States, the highest rates are found among American Indian and Alaska Native teens and young adults. In those groups, stress can arise when a young person's expectations and wishes clash with the traditional values of their culture or religion.

Young people who live in rural areas in countries such as China and India also have high rates of suicide. They may have difficulty finding work or

There is a high incidence of mental health problems among young offenders. They are more than twice as likely as adults to attempt suicide in prison.

CASE STUDY

Tia's family had moved to a new neighborhood when she was in 10th grade. At first, Tia felt awkward and had trouble making friends at a new school. Most of the students had formed cliques during the previous year, and Tia felt lonely. Then she met Rick. They started going out, and he introduced her to his friends. Rick had dropped out of school and had been in trouble with the police a few times.

Tia's parents disapproved of her relationship with Rick. After she came home past curfew for the third time, they told her she could no longer see him. They took away her cell phone and wouldn't let Rick speak to her when he called the house. Although Tia argued and pleaded, her parents were firm. At school, Tia's teachers noticed that she seemed anxious and depressed. Tia did not want to hurt her family, but she felt hopeless. One night, she attempted suicide by taking an overdose of painkillers. Tia's mother found her on the floor and called an ambulance.

homes. Family or relationship conflicts and the breakdown of traditional family structures and support may also be factors.

Other high-risk groups

High rates of suicide have been recorded among young people who are gay or lesbian. They may feel confused and isolated because of their sexuality. Many of them experience conflict within their families. Some are victims of bullying or violence.

Young people in prison or juvenile detention centers make up another high-risk group. In prison, people under the age of 21 have the highest suicide rate. Factors may include the existence of mood or behavior disorders and bullying by other inmates.

A genetic link?

Some experts think that the presence of a subform of one **gene** makes impulsive behavior and suicide more likely, but others disagree. Scientists in France and Switzerland recently reported that they had found a genetic variation that may be linked to suicide. Their research showed that the genetic alteration interfered with the brain's ability to produce a chemical that controls mood and anxiety levels.

Mood disorders and substance abuse

Overall, about 90 percent of suicides are linked to **mood disorders** or substance abuse. Young people, especially males, who abuse drugs or alcohol have high rates of suicide. One U.S. study of people under the age of 35 found that individuals with a history of drug abuse were five times as likely as others to die by suicide.

Deeper problems

Substance abuse is often the result of underlying problems, including depression and mood, personality, or anxiety disorders. Some young people take drugs or drink alcohol as a way of escaping difficult feelings. Alcohol and drugs affect the ability to think and reason. Some of these substances act as **depressants**, intensifying a mood of gloom and hopelessness. Drugs and alcohol can also reduce inhibitions and increase the risk of impulsive action. The National Strategy for Suicide Prevention estimates that half of people who die by suicide are **intoxicated** at the time. As many as one in five of them has used cocaine in the 24 hours before death.

Reacting to trauma

Many young people who have mood, personality, or anxiety disorders are reacting to traumatic events in their

Some distressed young people turn to substance abuse, such as inhaling solvents, to produce mind-altering effects and temporarily escape reality.

lives. Some may have been physically or sexually abused. Others may have gone through painful experiences such as family breakup.

Young people who have have had a family member, a classmate, or a friend who has committed suicide are at increased risk of suicidal thoughts and behavior. They may be experiencing unbearable grief and an overwhelming sense of loss. There is also a risk of copycat behavior. In rare instances, a suicide in a school or community can act as a trigger for other teens.

CASE STUDY

Josh started taking drugs when he was 14. At school, a gang of bullies was picking on him and making his life miserable. He felt depressed most of the time.

One day Josh was at a friend's house, where he was offered marijuana. He smoked it because he was curious. Smoking marijuana made him feel sick, but he also felt cool for doing it. He somehow felt that the bullies at school might respect him a bit more. Eventually, Josh began to feel that smoking marijuana was a means of escape. It made him feel calm and confident.

Josh went with a friend to a club, where he met a dealer. Josh started buying cocaine and Ecstasy regularly. He felt that getting high was the only good thing in his life, and he relied on drugs more frequently. At the same time, though, he felt more depressed. Josh was caught in a cycle that he thought he couldn't escape. Feeling trapped and hopeless, Josh took a drug overdose.

In focus: cluster suicides

In the United States, from 1 to 4 percent of suicides are "cluster" suicides carried out by peer groups. These are a series of suicides that happen closely together in terms of time and place.

Some cluster suicides have been triggered by an event or by a celebrity's suicide. For example, the death of rock star Kurt Cobain prompted a cluster of suicides among troubled fans. Cobain (1967–1994), the lead singer of the rock band Nirvana, had a long history of drug addiction. He was found dead at his home from a gunshot wound to the head.

Kurt Cobain

Suicide and antidepressants

Drug therapy is one approach to the treatment of depression and suicidal thoughts and behavior. Since the 1980s, antidepressants have been prescribed to an increasing number of young people.

Brain chemicals

Mental health experts believe that depression is a result of many factors, which may include an imbalance of certain chemicals in the brain. Different factors, such as stress and the genes people inherit from their parents, can lead to imbalances in these chemicals, which work to carry messages between the millions of brain cells.

The brain chemical **serotonin** is important in controlling mood, emotions, sleep, and body temperature. If a person's brain has too much serotonin at any time, he or she may feel sick and get headaches. A low level of serotonin can cause a person to feel depressed, lack energy and appetite, sleep poorly, and take little interest or pleasure in things around them.

Careful monitoring

Some antidepressant drugs, known as **selective serotonin reuptake inhibitors (SSRIs),** are thought to correct the imbalance of serotonin in the brain. Since being introduced, SSRIs have been prescribed to millions of people around the world.

SSRIs are sometimes prescribed for young people with moderate to severe depression. It is important that young people be carefully monitored when they are taking antidepressants, as some research studies suggest the medications may increase the risk of suicidal thoughts and behavior in a small number of young people.

Drug therapy can relieve the symptoms of depression in the short term.

Doctors prescribe antidepressants to children and teens on a case-by-case basis and are careful to assess patients regularly while they are taking the medications. Young patients are usually monitored every week during the first four weeks and regularly after that. Teens with depression may need to continue taking antidepressant medication for several months after they begin to feel better.

Drug therapy is not generally used to treat mild depression. When antidepressants are prescribed for young people, the medications are typically combined with other forms of therapy, such as counseling.

In focus: *serotonin*

The brain has many natural chemicals. The balance of these chemicals can be affected by genes, hormones, foods, alcohol, and other drugs. Levels of the "mood chemical" serotonin can be reduced if someone is under stress, eats a poor diet, or does not get enough exercise, sleep, or sunlight.

A well-rounded, nutritious diet and plenty of exercise, sleep, and time spent outdoors may enhance a person's mood.

Drug therapies are typically used in combination with other forms of therapy, such as individual counseling and group sessions.

Chapter 5: *Suicide prevention and therapy*

Some experts estimate that 80 percent of all people who attempt suicide want others to be aware of their intentions. In these cases, suicide may be a "cry for help." In many countries, suicide prevention programs train community workers, including teachers, school guidance counselors, social workers, and religious leaders, to recognize the warning signs of suicide. Of course, doctors and nurses are also trained to identify and support young people who are at risk of attempting suicide.

Warning signs

Warning signs that someone may be considering suicide can include a range of symptoms:

- loss of interest in hobbies, school, or work
- neglect of personal care and appearance
- giving away of prized possessions
- depression or anger
- withdrawal from friends and social activities
- difficulties eating and sleeping
- deliberately risky behavior

People with suicidal feelings may talk directly or indirectly about killing themselves. Sometimes they say they "want to end it all."

Regular individual counseling sessions can provide an outlet for young people to talk about their feelings and prevent problems from overwhelming them.

They may frequently mention death and dying or talk about the suicide of a friend or a famous person.

Getting help

People who show such symptoms need to speak with a trained individual who listens and encourages them to talk about their feelings. Suicidal teens may not have the mental or emotional energy to seek help alone, so they may need someone else to act for them. Crisis centers and helplines provide immediate support. Mental health professionals are also available to help.

Counseling and treatment

Treatment often begins with a visit to a family doctor. The doctor may then refer the young person to a specialist in mental health care. Children and teens who are suicidal need counseling to get through a time of crisis.

Longer-term talking therapies encourage troubled patients to deal with their negative feelings and behavior. In sessions, patients explore the causes of negative feelings, and therapists suggest appropriate techniques for manage those emotions. Patients may also need to be referred for clinical treatment of alcohol or drug abuse.

Some teens feel more comfortable talking to peer counselors. Peer

In focus: taking action

The SOS (Signs of Suicide) Program in U.S. high schools has led to a 40 percent reduction in suicide attempts in students who have been exposed to the program. Students are offered mental health checkups, and they watch a video that helps them recognize depression and suicidal thoughts in themselves and their friends. The program encourages them to ACT (Acknowledge, Care, and Tell).

If you have suicidal thoughts or think someone you know may be feeling suicidal, take action now. Talk to someone you know and trust, or call a crisis helpline. See page 47 for a list of organizations to contact.

counselors are young people trained to support other teens who are going through an emotional crisis and who need understanding and guidance.

New strategies are being developed to help prevent "cluster" suicides (see page 35) and to help young people cope with their strong feelings of grief and loss. These strategies can include one-on-one counseling, group counseling, information packs, and crisis helplines.

Suicide and the family

When people die by suicide, they leave behind family members and friends. These "suicide survivors" have to come to terms with the tragedy. They experience many feelings associated with sudden bereavement, such as shock, disbelief, sadness, and anger. Sometimes people continue to have painful memories of finding the body or learning of the suicide.

Suicide is especially difficult because a loved one has made the choice to die. Family and friends may blame themselves and feel guilty because they did not notice warning signs and weren't able to prevent the suicide. They may be confused and struggle to understand why their loved one chose to leave them. Bereaved parents, children, siblings, and other relatives often feel angry, hurt, and betrayed.

When a person dies by suicide, family members and friends may have difficulty coming to terms with the knowledge that their loved one chose to die.

Dealing with grief

People sometimes have trouble talking about suicide. Members within a family may respond differently, resulting in conflict or even family breakup. Surviving siblings can suffer because of their parents' preoccupation with the dead child. Some siblings become frightened and insecure or feel that they are being overprotected by an anxious parent. Siblings may feel resentment that a brother or a sister has upset or even destroyed their family. Because people sometimes avoid discussing suicide in front of children, siblings can feel isolated. They may start to have physical symptoms, such as stomachaches and headaches.

Coping strategies

It is important that all people affected by a suicide be able to talk openly about their feelings. It is natural to feel sorrow, anger, and loss. Burying those strong emotions can lead to problems such as chronic tiredness, depression, and physical illness. Experts believe that the body may deplete itself using energy to suppress strong emotions, rather than expressing them.

Keeping a journal and writing down feelings can be helpful. In addition to the support of family and friends, the help of a trained counselor or therapist may be needed. Support groups enable survivors to meet others who have experienced the suicide of a family member or a friend. Helplines can offer contact and support, too. Some people benefit from becoming actively involved in a suicide prevention program. They may feel that helping others gives some meaning to their own tragedies.

CASE STUDY

Darren was a conscientious student who worked hard at his studies. His goal was to someday become a doctor. When his girlfriend, Maria, ended their relationship, Darren began to feel depressed and under stress. He worried about his performance in school and became overwhelmed by a feeling of all-around failure.

One day, when he was at home alone, Darren ended his life by suicide. He left a note for his parents and Maria. Darren wrote that he was sorry he had let them all down and that they would be better off without him.

Darren's parents and Maria were devastated that they had not known about his depression. They blamed themselves for missing the signs. A social worker put them in touch with a suicide survivors' group. Darren's parents and Maria were helped by talking to other people who had experienced a similar tragedy.

Chapter 6: *Tackling the problem*

According to the World Health Organization, mental health disorders are the fourth leading cause of ill health worldwide. The group predicts that depression will be the world's second biggest health problem by 2020.

A global problem

Self-harm and depression are becoming more common among children and teenagers. Changes in society and family appear to be a related factor.

In some areas of the world, war, terrorism, poverty, and hunger are major causes of stress. Modern society can be characterized by a lack of time and attention given by parents. In addition, outdoor and creative play

In developing countries, poverty can be a cause of depression among young people.

have been largely replaced with entertainment from video and computer games.

Developing countries

Young people living in rural areas face new problems as traditional family and village structures break down and work becomes scarce. In some parts of developing countries, self-poisoning is a growing problem. About two-thirds of people who self-poison are younger than 30. They may use pesticides (farm chemicals), medicines, or natural poisons, such as oleander seeds. In China, Malaysia, Sri Lanka, and Trinidad, 60 to 90 percent of suicides involve pesticide poisoning.

Working together

International organizations such as the European Union and the United Nations are working to raise awareness of the problems of suicide and self-harm among young people. These groups want countries to work together to share resources and to consider the needs of children and teens in all mental health policies.

Some countries and states are considering new laws to restrict access to common methods of suicide. In Canada, stronger laws on the handling

In focus: children's well-being

In 2007, UNICEF released a report on the well-being of children around the world. The report included findings on children's satisfaction in their relationships with their family and friends, feelings of safety, and enjoyment of school.

Among the 21 countries surveyed, Portugal, Austria, Hungary, the United States, and the United Kingdom ranked among the lowest nations for children's well-being.

and storage of firearms resulted in a decrease of almost 40 percent in suicide by firearms. There are also calls for restrictions on package sizes of over-the-counter drugs and for safer storage of pesticides and other toxic substances. In places that attract suicides, such as bridges, the installation of emergency phones, fencing, and nets may discourage people from jumping.

More research projects are also needed to study suicide and self-harm in children and young people. The World Health Organization sponsors an annual World Suicide Prevention Day to raise awareness of this issue.

Supporting well-being

Young people today face many challenges in their lives that affect their physical and emotional health. Some factors, such as family breakup, are beyond their control. They can feel powerless to make changes, a situation that may damage their self-esteem.

Developing skills

Therapy for young people who self-harm aims to improve their self-esteem. It helps them find new ways of dealing with strong emotions and of controlling impulsive behavior. Programs help children and teens develop problem-solving skills and learn to communicate effectively.

Studies show that being in a supportive family and having stable relationships reduce the risk of suicide and self-harm. The risk of suicide is also reduced by other factors:

- lack of access to weapons, such as firearms
- commitment to religious or spiritual beliefs
- active participation in an organized religious community
- involvement in community events
- access to mental health care

Building self-esteem

Having self-esteem helps a person deal with everyday stresses and problems. People can improve their self-esteem by setting realistic goals and giving themselves credit when they achieve those goals. Thinking positively and challenging negative thoughts about themselves and events in their lives can

Having a network of supportive friends can build self-esteem and help young people cope during times of crisis.

also boost self-esteem. Some people are helped by recording in a journal or diary any positive events that happen during a day, such as performing well on a test or receiving a compliment.

Self-esteem is improved by having positive role models and a network of supportive friends. Some people make a list of things that cheer them up, such as a pet, a friend, a favorite place, or a happy holiday.

Other ways in which people can care for their physical and emotional health include exercising to release "feel good" endorphins, eating a healthful diet, and exploring new activities and interests. People who take care of themselves and accept themselves as they are have taken the first step in avoiding self-harm.

Pets can provide companionship and unconditional love, enhancing a person's feeling of well-being.

In focus: *school programs*

One strategy for improving well-being is through educational and counseling programs in schools. These programs are designed to help young people develop coping skills, especially in times of crisis. The Penn Resiliency Program provides children and teens with strategies to respond to the daily challenges and stresses they face during the middle and high school years.

Students take part in exercises designed to build optimism and encourage effective problem solving. The skills taught in the program can be applied to relationships with peers and family members as well as to achievement in school and other activities.

Glossary

acetaminophen: an over-the-counter medication that is commonly used to relieve pain and fever

acquired immune deficiency syndrome (AIDS): the final, life-threatening stage of infection with human immunodeficiency virus (HIV)

alcohol poisoning: a level of alcohol in the bloodstream that is high enough to cause unconsciousness, brain damage, and death

anorexia nervosa: an eating disorder in which people feel an extreme need to be thin. They have a distorted body image, abnormal eating patterns, malnutrition, and excessive weight loss.

antidepressants: medications taken to treat depression by altering the balance of chemicals in the brain

attention-deficit/hyperactivity disorder (ADHD): disordered learning and disruptive behavior that is characterized by inattentiveness, overactivity, or impulsive behavior

binge drinking: consumption of several drinks within a short period of time

body image: a person's mental picture of his or her body

bulimia nervosa: an eating disorder in which people binge on large amounts of food and then try to empty their bodies of the food, usually by vomiting or taking laxatives

depressants: substances, such as alcohol and some other drugs, that slow down bodily functions

depression: a mood disorder marked by persistent sadness, inactivity, difficulty in concentration, a significant increase or decrease in appetite and sleep, and feelings of hopelessness

detachment: indifference, separation, or lack of interest

eating disorders: a range of eating problems, including anorexia nervosa, bulimia nervosa, binge-eating disorder, and compulsive eating disorder

endorphins: chemicals in the brain that promote a feeling of well-being

gene: a very small part of a chromosome that influences inheritance and development of characteristics

genetic: produced by genes

hormones: chemicals formed in the body that control functions such as growth, development, and reproduction

human immunodeficiency virus (HIV): the virus that causes acquired immune deficiency syndrome (AIDS) by damaging the body's immune system

inhaling: breathing into the lungs

intoxicated: drunk; having mental and physical control diminished by alcohol

mood disorders: mental health problems, such as depression, that affect mood and well-being

obsessive-compulsive disorder (OCD): a mental disorder in which a person has obsessive thoughts and engages in compulsive behavior, such as repeated counting or handwashing

overdose: an amount of a drug that is greater than the recommended or prescribed dose

paranoia: a mental disorder in which a person is overly suspicious that others are watching or talking about him or her

physical abuse: physical mistreatment of one person by another

piercings: body decorations made by piercing the skin for jewelry

prescribed: ordered by a doctor as medical treatment

psychotherapy: treatment of mental or emotional disorders by psychological means

puberty: a series of physical changes that marks the end of childhood and the start of sexual maturity

schizophrenia: a mental illness in which people withdraw from reality and have illogical thoughts

selective serotonin reuptake inhibitors (SSRIs): antidepressant medications that regulate chemicals in the brain

self-esteem: confidence and satisfaction in oneself

serotonin: a chemical in the brain that is involved in controlling mood

sexual abuse: physical or sexual contact with a person against his or her will

tattoos: body decorations that are made using needles and pigments

tranquilizers: drugs used to reduce anxiety and tension

trauma: an event or experience that is very upsetting and shocking

Further information

Books to read

Crook, Marion. *Out of the Darkness: Teens Talk About Suicide.* Vancouver, Canada: Arsenal Pulp Press, 2004.

Kettlewell, Caroline. *Skin Game.* New York: St. Martin's Press, 2000.

Sperekas, Nicole B. *Suicide Wise: Taking Steps Against Teen Suicide (Teen Issues).* Berkeley Heights, N.J.: Enslow Publishers, 2000.

Wallerstein, Claire. *Teenage Suicide (Need to Know).* Chicago: Heinemann, 2003.

Winkler, Kathleen. *Cutting and Self-Mutilation: When Teens Injure Themselves (Teen Issues).* Berkeley Heights, N.J.: Enslow Publishers, 2003.

Organizations to contact

National Suicide Prevention Lifeline
Web site: **www.suicidepreventionlifeline.org**
Toll-free helpline: 1-800-273-TALK (8255)

The National Suicide Prevention Lifeline is a 24-hour suicide prevention service that provides immediate assistance to anyone in suicidal crisis. Callers are connected to the nearest available suicide prevention and mental health service provider. All calls are confidential.

Boys Town
Web site: **www.boystown.org**
Toll-free hotline: 1-800-448-3000

The Boys Town National Hotline is a 24-hour crisis, resource, and referral line. Trained counselors are available every day of the week, 365 days a year, to help teens with suicide and self-harm prevention.

Helpful web sites

American Association of Suicidology
www.suicidology.org

The American Association of Suicidology is an education and resource organization. Its site offers fact sheets on youth suicide and the link between suicide and depression, as well as current statistics and research findings.

National Alliance on Mental Illness (NAMI)
www.nami.org

NAMI provides information, referral, and education on mental health problems. The NAMI toll-free helpline is available Monday through Friday, 10 A.M. to 6 P.M. Eastern time. 1-800-950-NAMI (6264)

Suicide Awareness Voices of Education (SAVE)
www.save.org

The mission of SAVE is to prevent suicide through public awareness and education and to serve as a resource to those touched by suicide. The web site offers information on youth suicide; warning signs and symptoms; common misconceptions; and a depression checklist.

TeensHealth
www.kidshealth.org/teen/your_mind/ mental_health/suicide.html

TeensHealth (part of the KidsHealth web site) provides teenagers and families with accurate, up-to-date information about suicide and self-harm. Content is developed by doctors and other health experts.

Publisher's note to educators and parents: Our editors have carefully reviewed these web sites to ensure that they are suitable for children. Many web sites change frequently, however, and we cannot guarantee that a site's future contents will continue to meet our high standards of quality and educational value. Be advised that children should be closely supervised whenever they access the Internet.

Index